D A L L A S
CITY OF DREAMS

CITY OF DREAMS
THE PHOTOGRAPHERS OF *THE DALLAS MORNING NEWS*
TEXT BY KEVIN SHERRINGTON
FOREWORD BY GEORGE W. BUSH
INTRODUCTION BY ROGER STAUBACH
TAYLOR PUBLISHING COMPANY
DALLAS, TEXAS

Published by Taylor Publishing Company
1550 West Mockingbird Lane
Dallas, Texas 75235

Library of Congress Cataloging-in-Publication Data

Dallas: city of dreams / by the photographers of the Dallas morning
news; text by Kevin Sherrington.
p. cm.
ISBN 0-87833-708-3: $18.95
1. Dallas (Tex.) — Description — Views. I. Sherrington, Kevin.
F394.D243D35 1990 89-71362
976.4'2811 — dc20 CIP
Printed in the United States of America

10 9 8 7 6 5 4 3 2

Designed by Walter Gray Lamb

F O R E W O R D

DALLAS IS VERY MUCH a city of the future. It's a city that knows no limits, full of people who think big and act accordingly. We're proud of our heritage of bold initiative, and we stand poised before a future of unlimited potential.

FOR MORE THAN A CENTURY, Big D has been a destination for dreamers, a place where all kinds of people can make a better life for themselves. For, most of all, Dallas is a city of opportunity — a place where dreams can still come true.

GEORGE W. BUSH

INTRODUCTION

A QUIRK OF FATE brought me to Dallas in 1969, but the roots I have cultivated over the last twenty years have kept me here. This is where I have raised my family, created my business, formed close friendships, and joined in community activities. This is home.

DURING THE LAST twenty years, I have been a part of Dallas' cycles of recession and prosperity, but through it all, I have witnessed the prevailing themes of perseverance, teamwork, commitment to excellence, and civic pride. The competitive spirit that has been associated with Dallas since its pioneer days still burns strongly and is the catalyst that has once again brought Dallas into the limelight as the best place in the country to do business.

DALLAS HAS GROWN into a city that embodies the diverse needs and interests of all people. As we welcome new companies and their families relocating into our area, we offer them our excellent school and university systems; our professional sports; our fine arts museums and the new Morton Myerson Symphony Center; our first-rate shopping centers; and our park and recreational centers. But most of all, we want to share with them the winning spirit that will always be uniquely Dallas.

AS YOU TRAVEL through the following pages of *Dallas: City of Dreams,* perhaps you will also sense the pride we feel for our city.

Roger Staubach

ROGER STAUBACH

John Neely Bryan's life was not the stuff of which Disney movies are made. He came to Texas from Arkansas, contracted cholera, shot a man who had insulted his wife, hid in California for six years, was eventually committed to an asylum and died there, his remains left to be buried under some nameless marker. He did, however, found the city of Dallas — although he turned right around and sold it for $7,500.

Left: Aerial view of "Old Red," the Old Dallas County Courthouse

Preceding page: Egrets and other waterfowl take flight at a small pond.

Cattle drive on the banks of the Trinity River for the Republican National Convention

Bryan's municipal descendants would not have made the same mistake. But he had vision, if not fortune, when he rode up to a bluff overlooking the Trinity River one day in 1841 and said, "This is the place."

Bryan dug out a small, cramped hollow in the bluff — now Dealey Plaza near the southwest corner of downtown — and hunkered down with his dog and thoughts. At one time he may have been looking for a place to ply his trade with the Indians. But his customers had since been banished. He needed another plan now. He needed something grand.

Sculptor Martin Delabano repairs a 19th-century French sculpture at the Dallas Civic Garden Center in Fair Park.

He rallied with an idea that proved to be prophetic. The decision would be the single flare of genius in an unfortunate life, a bit of inspiration so stunning it eventually caught the town's imagination and grew until now, nearly 150 years later, it is Dallas' credo.

He put his newly acquired land up for sale.

Jogging along the levee of the Trinity River

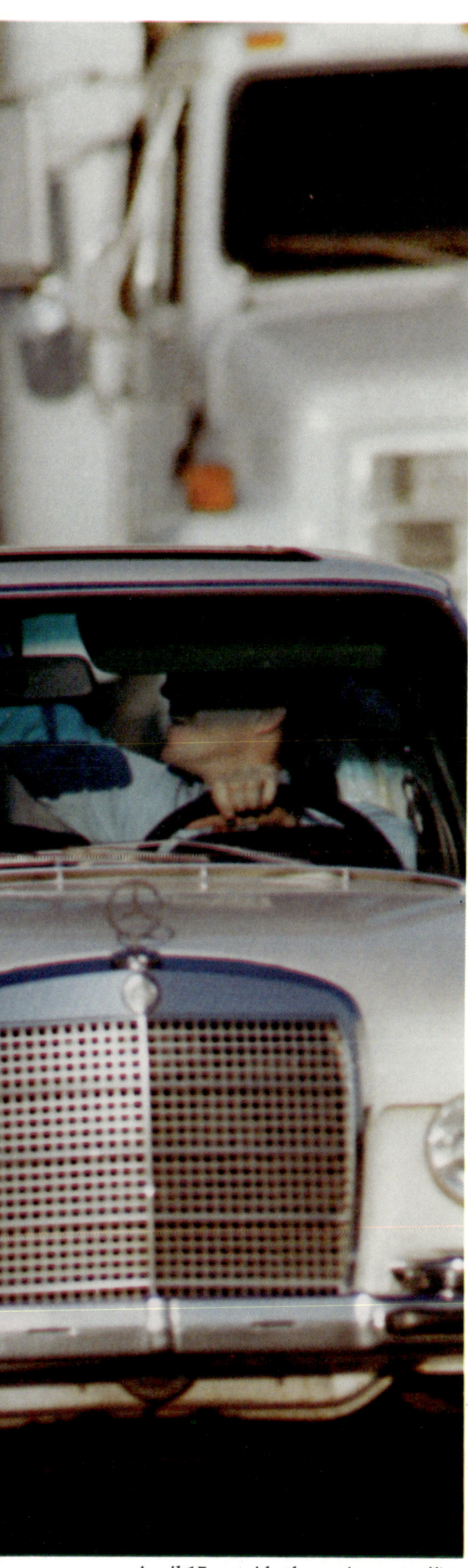

April 15 outside the main post office

Basically there was no other reason for Dallas except as an excuse to sell real estate. The pioneers' instinctive drive West already had reached past it. Fort Worth, a focal point of the Chisholm Trail, was down the road and doing quite nicely with its take of the cattle market when Bryan was rooting around the Trinity River banks.

Nothing of historical significance had happened here, as it had in San Antonio or Austin or Houston. The ground wasn't particularly fit for farming. Over the next 150 years, it would prove to be one of the few places in Texas where neither oil nor natural gas could be squeezed from a rock. Even the surrounding lakes are manmade.

Left: Dallas water fun

Right: White Rock Lake's sailboats

Adolphus Managing Director Jeff Trigger in the hotel's French Room

The outstanding physical characteristic of the area was that it was flat, which made it ideal for an airport. But Bryan's vision was not that acute. He had other transportation plans. He figured the Trinity could provide ideal access to the Gulf of Mexico, an idea embraced by all except the fickle river itself.

"Dallas," noted the late historian Herbert Gambrell, "is an example of a city that man has made, with a little help from nature and practically none from Providence."

Following page:
Cyclists in the Subaru Cycling Series speed around a downtown street corner.

What worked for Dallas where topography, minerals, and waterways failed was Bryan's abililty to sell it. To convince the early settlers, he used whiskey. Today, Greater Dallas business leaders carry on Bryan's spirit of business pluck with tax abatements, incentives, and a willingness to do the deal that has made Dallas a city of 1.4 million, the second-largest in the state and eighth-largest in the country.

The eclectic characters who helped shape the city in all its tentacled reaches — people such as Bryan, Sara Cockrell, H.L. Hunt, Leadbelly, R.L. "Bob" Thornton, Stanley Marcus, Father J. Von Brown, Ray Nasher, Mary Kay Ash, Ross Perot, and Tex Schramm — knew what would play and what wouldn't.

Former mayor Erik Jonsson, a man who shaped Dallas into a cosmopolitan presence

Left: Texas Rangers third baseman Steve Buechele

Right: Kids enjoying the ballgame at Arlington Stadium

The city's commitment to the arts, fashion, sports, good newspapers, high property values, and the best Mexican food within a two hundred-mile radius has made Dallas one of the most livable areas in the country.

No other Texas city has done more with less.

No other Texas city had a better handle on why.

The differences between Dallas and Fort Worth, or Dallas and Houston, Austin, and San Antonio are not so subtle. Houston is an international port, a "Sweat City" built by air conditioning and with little feel for the cultural grit of Texas despite its place in Texas independence. Austin, the San Diego of Texas, is an artist colony with a political bent. And despite its size, San Antonio, home of the Alamo, still lives in Austin's shadow.

Fort Worth, though just twenty-eight miles from Dallas, could not be more different. "Cowtown," a label worn with pride, is the world's biggest small town. Dallas, in effect, is the world's smallest city.

Checking out police equipment

34
22

Left: Dallas Maverick Rolando Blackman drives for a basket.

Right: Tatu battles for the ball during a Dallas Sidekick playoff game.

Dallas has the requisite night spots: Lower Greenville Avenue near the center of town, Deep Ellum off downtown, the West End downtown, and Restaurant Row in far northwest Dallas. It has The Galleria and NorthPark, two of the finest shopping malls in Texas. It has or shares major league football, baseball, basketball, and soccer teams. It has a national reputation in fashion and business. It even has a song and a catchy nickname.

What it does not have, however, is sheer size.

Left: A Dallas park

Right: Curved beds of tulips and pansies at Dallas Blooms in the Arboretum

Traversing Dallas is easy once you learn every main artery has at least two names and neither has anything to do with the direction it travels.

R.L. Thornton, for instance, is really Interstate 30, a belt under the belly of downtown connecting Fort Worth with East Texas. LBJ is Loop 635, which runs around the top of Dallas and down its east side. Stemmons, or Interstate 35, starts north and hangs down the west side of Dallas, tumbling out underneath to begin a long, flat ride through Central Texas.

Following page: A cluster of swimming pools in the suburbs

Dead in the center of Dallas and cleaving it into East-West hemispheres is Highway 75, also known as Central Expressway, or the world's longest, skinniest parking lot. The expressway, the state's oldest and built before anyone knew better, is undergoing a facelift to facilitate better traffic flow.

Dallas freeway traffic has many destinations. A host of bedroom communities — Plano, Richardson, Garland, Mesquite, Irving, Duncanville, DeSoto, Carrollton, Las Colinas, Grand Prairie, Addison, and Farmers Branch, to name a few — press hard on all sides of Dallas. Arlington, home of the Texas Rangers and Six Flags, has done so well as a buffer between Fort Worth and Dallas that it has become a sizeable city of its own.

Left: Sculpture, Las Colinas

Right: Bronze mustangs thunder through Williams Square at Las Colinas.

Despite Central, traffic in the city is modest, at best. Complainants are sent to Houston, where they quickly learn the time-space relationship of why people age faster in an automobile.

Buses, some inexplicably with ears, are everywhere in Dallas. Stand still anywhere on a downtown sidewalk and a bus is liable to roar up to your feet. There also is talk of going to a type of rail system for commuter traffic, which would be appropriate for a city that owes its growth to the fact that it was able to talk, or finagle, two railroad lines to intersect in Dallas and thus turn it from a small, flat town into a transportation hub.

Civic leaders in 1872 put together a few thousand dollars, 115 acres, and several miles of free right-of-way as incentive for officials of the Houston and Texas Central to lay down tracks just east of Dallas, or what is now Central Expressway. The transformation of Dallas was completed when, not long after, town officials convinced the Texas legislature to attach to a bill a codicil requiring the Texas and Pacific, running east and west, to pass within a mile of Browder Springs, now the site of Old City Park south of downtown.

Preceding page: A young ice skater practices her spins at the ice rink of the Plaza of the Americas Hotel.

Right: Ron Ellis' world-class Frisbee dog, Maggy

The railroads that gave Dallas its heartbeat eventually died. But Dallas didn't. Other modes of transportation replaced the railroads. Formerly a military air base, Love Field became the city's minicipal airport, and when Dallas outgrew it, Dallas/ Fort Worth International was built between the two cities. DFW has become one of the country's most frequently used airports, as anyone who has made a flight with two or more connections can confirm.

Left: An eclipse over downtown Dallas

Right: Clouds move across the skyline

One of the benefits of Dallas' place on the prairie is the view of its skyline. The colors of a slow, brilliant sunset reflecting off the mirrored buildings is one of the best excuses for being caught downtown near nightfall.

The Dallas skyline, though humble in most respects, is unmistakable for three of its more gaudy symbols: the futuristic green outline of the NCNB Bank building, the lighted "dandelion" crown of Reunion Tower, and the fifty-year-old "Flying Red Horse" atop the Magnolia, or Mobil, Building. The horse, which for twenty years sat atop the tallest building in Dallas and was recognizable for miles, is now nearly hidden among a forest of glass redwoods.

Following page: The McKinney Avenue Trolley

369

The rest of downtown Dallas basically can be divided into five areas.

Deep Ellum, a historic bed of jazz and blues, lies just east of Central Expressway off Elm; the West End, a fashionable gaggle of restaurants and nightclubs, actually is in the northwest; the Arts District occupies the northeast; the Farmers Market area is in the southeast; and the Convention Center, which includes Reunion Arena, fills out the southwest. All of the areas are evidence of city planners' desires to slow urban decay.

TILT
BUY ANY GAME IN THE STORE!
Holiday Sale!
GREAT Family GIFT
SEE ATTENDANT FOR DETAILS PRICES SUBJECT TO VERIFICATION
Dallas Alley

Left: Dallas Alley in the West End Marketplace, one of many refurbished warehouses in the West End Historic District in downtown Dallas

Right: July 4, Dallas style

The West End has proven to be a particular boon in the 1980s. Old brick warehouses that once were the centers of commerce were cleaned out and given a facelift. The result is an intimate series of night spots and restaurants ranging from Italian to Chinese to Mexican that make it possible for patrons to park and easily walk from one establishment to the next.

Deep Ellum at night

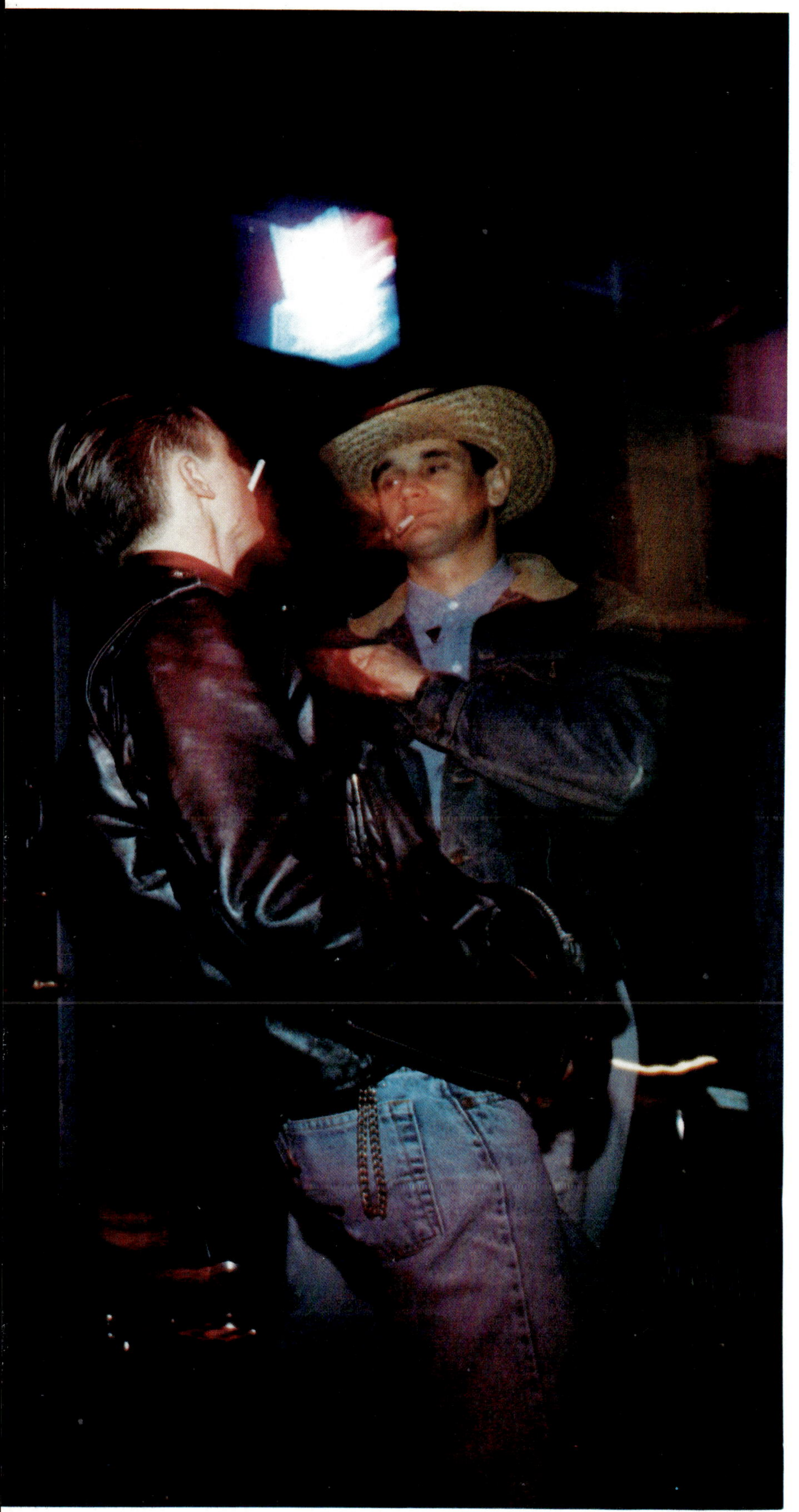

The other end of the downtown entertainment spectrum is Deep Ellum, which once claimed the likes of blues players Leadbelly and "Blind Lemon" Jefferson and, of late, folk-rockers Edie Brickell and New Bohemians.

Dark and hip, Deep Ellum has been made over in recent years for a younger crowd mostly unaware of its rich history. Originally one of the Freedmen Towns that sprang up after the Civil War, Deep Ellum was a place where African-Americans lived by their own rules. The music they created and the secret life they led in a segregated Southern city surely was one of white Dallas' losses. The area had all but died with the building of Central Expressway in 1949 until a new generation of musicians discovered it, at least preserving one aspect of its heritage.

Left: Rangers pitcher Nolan Ryan throws his 5,000th career strikeout.

Right: At Arlington Stadium, 40,907 opening-night fans watch the Rangers.

African-Americans have much to cherish in their Dallas history. Maynard Jackson, a local pastor, was the father of the man of the same name who would one day become mayor of Atlanta. Attorneys W.J. Durham and C.B. Bunkley, Jr. litigated hundreds of civil rights cases, many in conjunction with NAACP attorneys such as Thurgood Marshall, now a Supreme Court justice. They fought for the admission of African-Americans to university law schools and changed injustices such as "Negro Day" at the State Fair, a practice that limited African-Americans to one day at the Fair.

One of Dallas' most colorful African-American leaders was Father J. Von Brown, the handsome, hypnotic pastor of the Lighted Church of Prayer on the corner of Warren and Myrtle. Father Brown's church, which combined elements of Catholicism and Protestantism, numbered five thousand members at the height of his popularity in the late 1950s. He rode in a chauffeured Cadillac and was attended by women he referred to as "angels." Despite his social station, he ran afoul of the law a few times and was arrested once for failing to vacate his church.

He became ill in jail in 1965 and died enroute to the hospital, a fact that did not deter his followers. Father Brown had promised to rise again in three days, and his body was not buried until he had a chance to fulfill that promise. Attending "angels" fanned his brow in anticipation. Apparently, however, he was not up to a resurrection.

Left: Dallas Blooms at the Dallas Arboretum

Following page: Urban art is increasingly part of the cityscape.

MERCANT

The M-20 National Championship Regatta at Lake Ray Hubbard

Historians have said this is a town run discreetly by women, and they also can claim a strong legacy.

The first person to become a millionaire in Dallas was a woman — Sara Cockrell, the widow of the man who bought John Neely Bryan's lots. Mrs. Cockrell took the money her husband left her and built an empire, although she was careful to list men as the heads of her various businesses so as not to offend the sensibilities of those males who contributed to her fortune.

Left: Some of the more than 300 species of bromeliads, ferns, and other native South American plants in the Neotropical Walk-Through Aviary

Right: The Neotropical Walk-Through Aviary in the Bird and Reptile House at the Dallas Zoo

Other women were just as successful. Belle Starr became one of America's most famous criminals. Annette Strauss became mayor. Ela Hockaday established one of the most well-respected girls' schools in the country. Mary Kay Ash made a fortune out of the cosmetics business and Ebby Halliday took a small real estate firm on the corner of Preston and Northwest Highway and made it into one of the state's most successful. H.L. Hunt's daughters greatly increased their inheritances while their brothers for the most part squandered a great deal of theirs.

The Pepsi Hoop-It-Up in downtown

Businesses like to call Dallas home. The city is the birthplace, among others, of 7-Eleven, Haggar, Steak and Ale, Frito-Lay, Chili's, Black-Eyed Pea, and Texas Instruments, and the adopted home of any number of other national corporations.

This diversity kept Dallas from going under during the oil bust, as most of the rest of Texas did. But the city's place in the oil industry is shared by association, if not dependence. And the primary reason for that was H.L. Hunt.

SPALDING

Hunt's life would have made a good soap opera. He told one reporter he fathered seventy-eight children. An SMU professor said Hunt paid for the tuition of twenty-one of them. He was known to have two legal wives and at least one mistress, probably a highly conservative estimate.

Like John Neely Bryan, Hunt came to Texas from Arkansas. He became what one magazine considered the richest man in the country because of an East Texas oil field that proved, at the time, to be the biggest strike in history.

Dallas Maverick Derek Harper fights for a rebound during the Mavericks' first NBA playoff appearance.

Martina Navratilova at the Virginia Slims

His fortune enabled him to give his many offspring a nice headstart in life, which, to their credit, they have not sat upon. Lamar became a sports entrepreneur, founding the Kansas City Chiefs (originally the Dallas Texans) and World Championship Tennis and funneling much of his money to soccer. Bunker repeated his father's legacy in oil while creating a name for himself in the horse world. Caroline is a hotel magnate whose Dallas holdings have included The Crescent (one of Dallas' most ambitious restaurant/hotel/ office space consortiums) and The Mansion on Turtle Creek (perhaps the city's most elegant restaurant and hotel). Reunion Tower is also part of the Hunt real estate empire.

A Memorial Day Hot Air Balloon rally

Despite his wealth and appetites, H.L. Hunt was little known in Dallas until his picture appeared one day in 1948 in *Life.* The caption asked if this was the richest man in America. If he wasn't, you probably couldn't have lived long on the difference.

His widow, Ruth, still lives in the elegant mansion on White Rock Lake, one of the more scenic spots in Dallas. The lake once was a creek until it was dammed and is now a haven for sailing, cycling, and jogging.

Left: An okapi moves freely within the Wilds of Africa.

Right: The gorilla habitat includes a field research station in the Wilds of Africa exhibit.

Lakewood, the area surrounding White Rock Lake, is one of the city's more fashionable neighborhoods — although the stature of neighborhoods in Dallas has fluctuated over the years.

The first posh area of Dallas, now the site of I-30, was called the Cedars, just south of downtown. The last reminder of what another elegant neighborhood, Ross Avenue, used to look like before downtown grew up is the Belo Mansion, once owned by the founder of *The Dallas Morning News*, A.H. Belo. Swiss Avenue, a strip of vintage splendor just east of downtown between Live Oak and Gaston, took firm root again in the 1980s after a period of decline. The Swiss Avenue Historic District Association has ensured the preservation of the wide, grand homes.

Following page: Sun-worshipping turtles at Bachman Lake

Munger Place, a twenty-block area of prairie-style homes noted for wide porches and many gables, also has been restored, as has the Junius Heights area. The proximity to downtown and the unique, older homes appeal to the homeowners in these East Dallas areas. The homes can be seen inside out each Mother's Day weekend, when the Swiss Avenue Historic District conducts a tour of homes.

Opposite: Light plays an important part in Dallas architecture.

Left: One Dallasite's approach to interior decorating reflects the region's interest in the outdoors.

Right: Many Dallas homes juxtapose classical elements with frontier touches.

Left: Many of the city's estates incorporate fountains and pools into their landscape design.

Right: Christmas elegance

But of all the areas that make Dallas the most expensive real estate, per capita, in Texas, the richest area is not actually in Dallas.

Highland Park and University Park are independent islands in the center of Dallas, a mixture of old, sprawling homes on huge lots and new, sprawling homes on tiny lots. The two towns, or Park Cities, have independent city governments and services, although most of the leading citizens are the power brokers of Dallas.

 A pep rally in front of Dallas Hall on the Southern Methodist University campus

The area is roughly bounded to the west and east by the Tollway and Central, with Northwest Highway and Lemmon Avenue the primary boundaries north and south. The area includes Highland Park Village on Mockingbird and Preston, the oldest shopping center in the country (opening 1931). Southern Methodist University sits just west of Central. Preston Road, which runs through the heart of the Park Cities, is, indeed, the oldest street in Dallas, older, in fact, than the city itself. John Neely Bryan reportedly was riding down Preston Trail when he ran into the bluff on the banks of the Trinity.

The Mercedes Grand Prix Southwest Jumping Championships at Las Colinas

Highland Park citizens also have a keen insight into their civic duty, in more ways than one. At Christmas time this city becomes one of the most popular tourist attractions in Dallas after transforming its hundred-year-old pecans into "Sugar Plum Trees" of lights and giving horse-and-carriage rides to holiday merrymakers.

The M-20 National Championship Regatta at Lake Ray Hubbard

Bonnie Parker and Clyde Barrow were young, deadly, and the most famous outlaws of their time.

They also were Dallasites.

They lived in Dallas before and during their two-year crime spree, which ended in 1934 near Arcadia, Louisiana. They had been popular in the media, a fact that Bonnie particularly enjoyed. She once sent a poem to a newspaper that became a sort of simple-minded legacy:

Some day they'll go down
together,
They'll bury them side by side.
To few it'll be grief
To the law a relief
But it's death for Bonnie
and Clyde.

From the high-drive platform at the University of Texas at Arlington, a bird's-eye view of the McDonald's Junior Olympic Swimming Classic

Bonnie was right about the dying but wrong about the burying. Their bullet-riddled bodies were brought back to Dallas and the ensuing funerals produced lines around the block. Refreshments were sold. Overflying planes dropped flowers.

But crime's favorite couple were not buried side by side. They occupy plots in Dallas cemeteries across town from each other.

Local hero Kevin Von Erich applies the "Iron Claw" to World Champion Ric Flair in a title match at Texas Stadium.

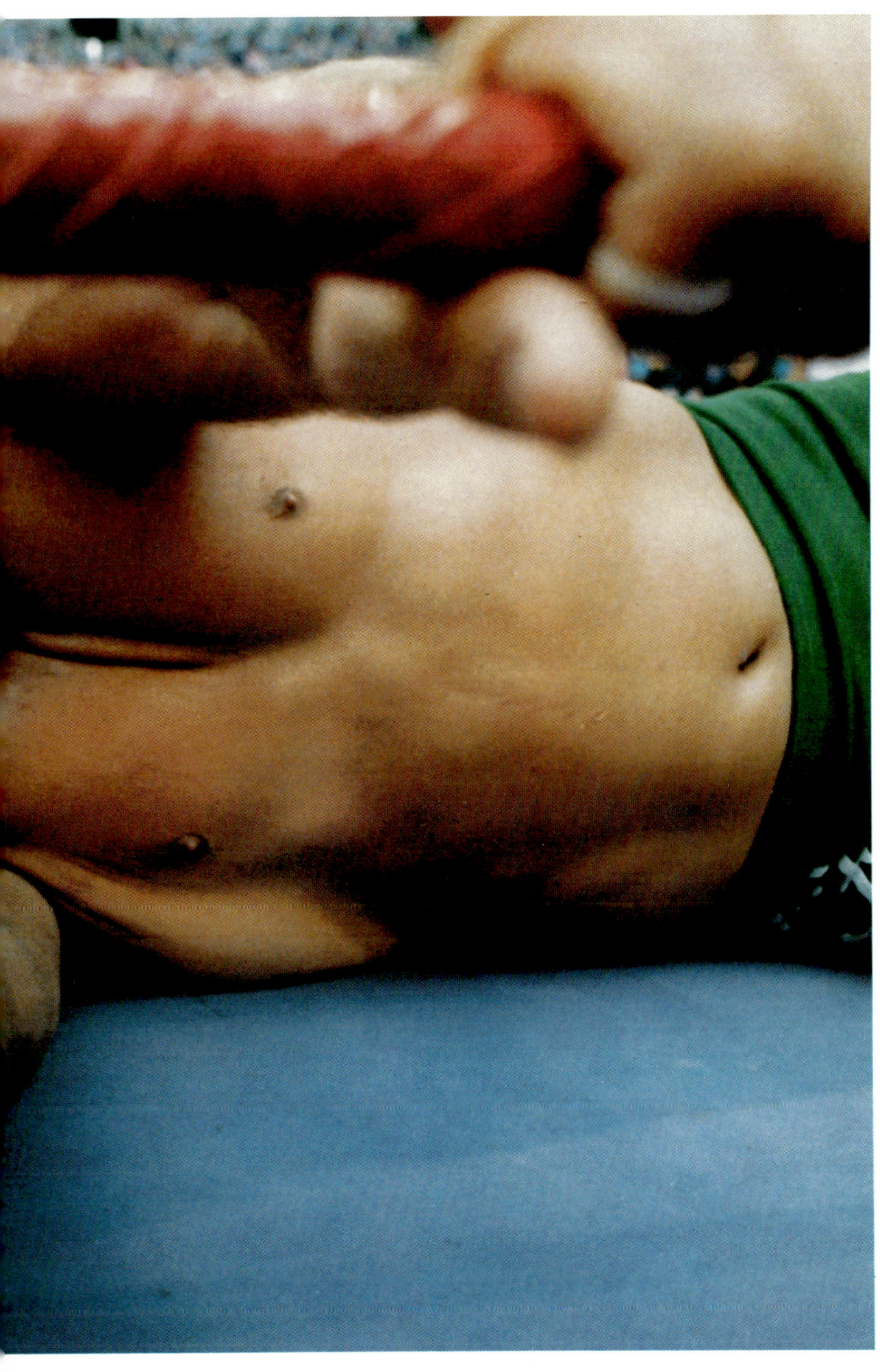

Dallas' most famous criminal was a man who hadn't lived in the area very long. Lee Harvey Oswald had lived lots of places, including the USSR, but he made his mark in Dallas.

A national image of Dallas as a center of right-wing intolerance had been brewing for three years when John F. Kennedy's motorcade took a ride down Houston on November 22, 1963, and turned left on Elm. What happened at that point was the shocking culmination of a series of nasty public incidents that, for many years, colored the world's perception of Dallas.

Following page: The GTE Byron Nelson Classic

The sixth-floor perch of the old Texas School Book Depository building, where Oswald fired his fatal shots at President Kennedy, has been converted after much municipal soul-searching into a museum. The site, despite its change of ownership to Dallas County, had remained much as it was when Oswald left it and, a few days later, was killed himself by Dallas nightclub owner Jack Ruby.

The John F. Kennedy Memorial in downtown

Preceding page: A view of the Kennedy assassination site from the Texas School Book Depository, now the Sixth Floor Museum

The rest of the area remains unchanged as well: Dealey Plaza (John Neely Bryan's old campsite), the triple underpass, and the "grassy knoll" — from which some witnesses claimed another shot was fired.

Much of the nation has not gotten over the fact that Kennedy was shot in Dallas. The city itself was slow in recovering. But The Sixth Floor Exhibit, as well as a downtown memorial to Kennedy that sits across the square from what is purported to be John Neely Bryan's first cabin, is an eloquent response to this terrible national loss.

Zebras in the Dallas Zoo's Wilds of Africa exhibit

Culture long ago came to Texas and tried to make a go of it in Dallas. It initially failed as a working concept but left an enduring impression.

Perusing the works at Artfest

Making bubbles at Fair Park's Science Place

La Reunion, a French colony, was founded in 1854 in an area that, at the time, was just south of Dallas. The inhabitants were philosophers, painters, music lovers, poets — in all, not a very hardy lot for the times. They made great conversation but, unfortunately, very little money. By 1867, the colony was extinct. Some went back to Europe; others moved to Dallas and integrated with the locals. But they left Dallas with a distinct appreciation for the arts that continues today.

The Morton Meyerson Symphony Hall makes a dramatic nighttime statement.

Ray Nasher, who built NorthPark Center, has been one of the city's leading proponents of art. A host of playwrights, including Pulitzer Prize-winners Beth Henley (*Crimes of the Heart*) and Donald Coburn (*The Gin Game*), lived and worked in Dallas. The new Morton Meyerson Symphony Center, in northeast downtown, is ranked by its backers as one of the finest music halls in the country.

Left: The interior of the Morton Myerson Symphony Hall

Right: Dallas Dance Festival on the plaza of the Dallas Museum of Art

As the downtown skyline testifies, Dallas likes its architecture bold and unusual. Internationally renowned architect I. M. Pei designed both the Morton Meyerson Symphony Center and Dallas City Hall. And one of Frank Lloyd Wright's final triumphs is the Dallas Theater Center's Kalita Humphries Theater, a Guggenheim-like structure nestled on the banks of Turtle Creek.

Most of the city's artistic pursuits, notes Dallas historian and journalist A.C. Greene, can be traced to La Reunion. Greene contends that the aesthetic think-tank gave Dallas its genesis as a cosmopolitan center.

Some say it was the Mexican food.

Or maybe it was the idea of selling Dallas.

Left: A Ballet Folklorico dancer celebrates Cinco de Mayo.

Following page: Ready for the rodeo

Left: A cowboy grabs for the tail of a bull in an effort to beat the clock at a Charreada.

Right: "Repo Man" at the Mesquite Rodeo

The State Fair is a perfect example of that idea. The fair had been a Dallas staple for years and comfortably profitable. But when the Texas Centennial celebration was being planned for 1936, R.L. "Bob" Thornton had bigger ideas for the area east of downtown.

Brian Hawks dismounts "Bojangles" at the Walt Garrison All Star Rodeo.

Thornton, one of the most powerful men in Dallas history, was just the man to make something big happen. He was a four-term mayor of Dallas. Even more impressive, for nearly half this century he headed the Citizens' Council, a back-scenes group of Dallas businessmen who helped to shape policy in Dallas, mostly for its good.

Paleontologist Kyle Davies reconstructs the remains of a 220-foot tenontosaurus for the Museum of Natural History at Fair Park.

Thornton's idea was to win the bid for the Centennial bash away from Houston, San Antonio, and Austin. A contingent was sent to the capital bearing gifts and promises if the Centennial was awarded to Dallas. Among the promises were the State Fair site, $10 million in cash and property, and assurances that museums, an amphitheater, and an aquarium would be built.

Dallas, as usual, sold itself. Fair Park became the site of the Centennial and, in the process, became one of the state's top attractions. Big Tex, the red, white, and blue cowboy welcoming visitors at the gate, became a symbol of Dallas.

Waiting for the head of Big Tex as the 56-foot mascot is readied for the opening of the State Fair of Texas

Left: The Texas State Fair ends with the dismantling of Big Tex.

Left: Along the festive Midway at night

Right: Getting some rest at the Fair's livestock show

Dallas wasn't finished selling, however. One of the outgrowths of Fair Park was the Cotton Bowl, which was built to provide a forum for a New Year's football game each year. The idea was to have the Southwest Conference champion play a worthy opponent to a packed house. But the first two SWC champions went elsewhere. So Cotton Bowl officials did the logical thing: they forged an agreement with the SWC binding the league champion to the Cotton Bowl, thus preserving its future.

COTTON BOWL
COTTON BOWL
BUSCHHHH!
Pizza Pizza

The only other game played in the Cotton Bowl now is the annual Texas-Oklahoma rivalry. It's played on an October weekend amid great fanfare that usually outdoes the game.

An aerial view of the Texas-Oklahoma rivalry at the State Fair

Left: The Cowboys' Manny Hendrix tackles an opponent.

Right: Cowboys owner Jerry Jones spends his first day at training camp.

The Cowboys used to play in the Cotton Bowl but have long since moved to Irving's Texas Stadium, although that could change any day at the whim of Jerry Jones, a former Arkansas Razorback who bought the team, fired Tom Landry, and hasn't settled down since. He has created quite a stir in a city used to strong-willed owners such as the Texas Rangers' Brad Corbett and Eddie Chiles or the Mavericks' Donald Carter.

BJ
118

COWBOYS
EAGLES
21
QTR
TO GO
Airlines
Winston
Coke

Left: A full house at Texas Stadium

Right: A Dallas Cowboys Cheerleader

Preceding page: The Dallas Cowboys at Texas Stadium

Jones, however, has no peers in raising a ruckus. He took a team that was an institution in Dallas and turned it upside down. No one else had come in and taken Dallas by its white collar since, well, since the last two guys who came here by way of Arkansas, H.L. Hunt and John Neely Bryan.

Ultimately Jones got his way. The city finally acquiesced because Jerry Jones proved he had the vision and purpose to succeed — like so many in the history of Dallas. It is in the city's affable nature to play up to anyone of power or fame.

"Dallas is not a secret city," wrote A.C. Greene. "Minneapolis, Denver, San Diego — they are not mystery cities. They, like Dallas, are open, eager to please, to be known, and to know. Their history is in the front of the book, there are no ancient burial grounds, no hidden gardens or antique lives lived behind bulfinch facades or tall wrought-iron gates. Dallas wants you to know it, to like it."

Getting a thrill on The Conquistador at Six Flags Over Texas

Life imitates art in the Arts District during a February rainstorm

Dallas has proven it will take anyone who has something to offer.

But it should be wary, perhaps, of anyone else coming from Arkansas.

Photo Credits

William Snyder 24-25, 64, 98, 100

Paula Nelson 12, 26, 32, 33, 49, 52, 58, 62, 82, 90, 101, 125

Judy Walgren 66, 94, 113, 118, 126

Erich Schlegel 22, 48, 50, 78, 88-89, 119

Michael S. Wirtz 28

Evans Caglage 53, 70, 71

David Woo 29, 34, 38, 104-105, 116, 123

Jan Sounenmair 84, 86, 107

David Leeson 14, 30, 45, 46, 56-57, 92, 108, 114

Juan Garcia 18, 39, 40-41, 68, 72-73, 106, 112, 115

Catharine Krueger 60, 61, 81, 96, 110

Randy Eli Grothe 8-9, 16, 43, 96

Lon Cooper 10, 20, 21, 36, 74, 75, 76, 77, 102

Cindy Yamanaka 35, 54

Ken Geiger 44